KID STARS RISING

KID STARS RISING

The Adventures of Rosebud Middle School

Sharonne Simmons, Ed.D.
Illustrated by David L. Simmons

XULON PRESS

Xulon Press
2301 Lucien Way #415
Maitland, FL 32751
407.339.4217
www.xulonpress.com

Printed in the United States of America.

ISBN-13: 978-1-54564-869-8

Table of Contents

Chapter 1

The Stars of Rosebud Middle School

A group of students are about to emerge at Rosebud Middle School that may be unlike any that you have ever met before. For Kai, Isabella, Jacob, Sophia, David, Kendall, and Dolores, it would be an unlikely adventure, a meeting of minds that they would never imagine in their wildest dreams. This is mainly due to their different races, backgrounds, and cultures. The experiences they encounter will bring them together. We will meet all of them in this book.

The first day of school at Rose Bud Middle School in Bear Creek, North Carolina was quickly approaching. Many students were very excited about meeting one another. Some were a little anxious because it was their first time at a new school. So many things to worry about: Will I make friends? Will I like my new teachers, and will they like me? Are my clothes acceptable to the others? Where are all my classes? How much time do I have between classes to go to my locker and get to my next class? These are just a few of the questions running through their heads on the first day of school.

The first day of school started off beautifully. Principal Johnson and her staff were ready to hit the ground running and make Rosebud Middle School the best school in the district. Rosebud Middle School was located in the suburban area of Bear Creek, North Carolina. It was a fairly large school, containing sixty classrooms and a huge gym. Providing softball, baseball, volleyball, track and field, soccer, basketball, tennis, and wrestling, it was known for its comprehensive sports program. Rosebud Middle School was surrounded by a host of affluent family-owned businesses, popular restaurants, several churches, and a public library. Bear Creek was a highly sought-after school district due to its mix of middle-class neighborhoods and one very wealthy neighborhood which included a golf course. Of course, Bear Creek contained a creek where families could fish and hold special events for a small rental fee. The families that lived in Bear Creek were proud of where they lived and protected their neighborhoods with community watch programs.

Chapter 2

Forming New Friendships

The first day of school at Rose Bud Middle was a plethora of hustle and bustle. Everyone was in search of their new classrooms, while new students needed to find their lockers. The Principal, Mrs. Johnson, was positioned front and center in the main lobby greeting students as they arrived at school. Principal Johnson was a middle-aged, tall African-American lady with a sweet face. Her clothes were chic and classy, and her hair was in a smart bob. She was slender and demure but carried a commanding presence about herself. Her calming demure eased the tension for many of the students.

The assistant principal, Mr. Rains, was an average built white man who wore glasses and sported a long black beard. He looked like he was about forty years old. Both administrators loved their students and wanted to ensure that they were open to help the students in any way they could. Once all of the students were settled into their classes, the principal and assistant principal walked around to introduce themselves to the students.

Several other teachers and staff served as guides to assist new students in finding their way to the cafeteria for breakfast or their classrooms. Since Kai, Kendall, and Dolores were sixth graders, they were part of the group of students who had the paradoxical emotions of nervousness and excitement. They did not know what to expect, so anticipation was at the root of their existence.

As they searched for their classes, Kai noticed that many of the students were familiar with the teachers, asking them for advice and discussing this past summer's adventures. That's when he thought, *I must be in the wrong hall.*

A tall, slim, handsome blonde-haired boy approached him and said, "Hey there. Are you lost?"

Kai gave a resounding, yet relieved, "Yes."

"What class are you looking for?" the handsome blonde-haired, blue eyed, well-dressed student asked.

Kai answered, "Mr. Yen's Biology 101."

"Follow me," replied the handsome young man. "I have that same class, too. By the way, my name's Jacob, what's yours?"

Kai replied, "Kai Kem. I'm new here. Always lived in Bear Creek, but just moved recently to this school district for sixth grade."

Jacob Wentworth extended his hand. "Nice to meet you, Kai. I'm in the seventh grade."

Jacob was used to helping new students. In fact, he was part of a peer mediation group that several teachers and the assistant principal created last year. Jacob was chosen because he had a calm and cool demeanor that attracted those who were fearful and unsure. Jacob was a teacher's favorite and many a girls' dream boyfriend.

Jacob is the seventh-grade quintessential stud. At twelve, he is a handsome blonde with blue eyes, well-dressed, athletic, smart, and to just about everyone he meets, plain out right cool. His dad is in the special forces and his mother is a stay-at-home soccer mom who is very supportive of his six-year old sister Kara and him during their soccer events. Jacob plays soccer very well. He won several MVP awards for helping the school team score during the final minutes of the game. Kara is following in his footsteps, and Jacob is very proud of this.

The Wentworth Family lives in Bear Creek in one of the more upscale neighborhoods in the Rosebud Middle School district. When it comes to school, sometimes Jacob can get lazy, especially because learning comes easy to him. It took him little to no effort to make top grades in some of the most challenging subjects in middle school. Dubbed academically-gifted in both math and reading, his teachers adore his intelligence, sense of humor, and quick wit. Jacob is often the subject of many a girl's dreams in a boyfriend. He has a way with the girls, and he shows no coyness in displaying this talent.

Kai is a Hawaiian-American eleven-year old seventh-grader. Kai has two twin three-year old brothers, Reece and Royce, who take much of their parents' time as three-year-olds do. His parents came from Honolulu right before he was born, and his maternal grandparents came to live with them when he was six years old.

The Kems live in the suburbs of Bear Creek, North Carolina. Kai attended Winding Creek Middle School last school year. His parents decided to have Kai change to Rosebud Middle School because the school was closer to his twin brothers' daycare for driving convenience.

Kai loves his little brothers but wished that he could have more of his parents' affection. When the boys were born, Kai noticed that all the special attention he once received was shifted quickly to the boys. His grandparents, however, try very hard to spread the love throughout all of them with no partiality. He didn't blame his parents. They were very busy all the time. His mother is a stay-at-home mom who keeps the home very clean and ensures that they always have a hot meal on the table every evening. His dad is an aeronautics engineer who works long hours, even some weekends. His grandparents played a large part in raising Kai and will help him as he makes his transition to middle school.

Now meet Kendall McSwain. Kendall is a beautiful dark-skinned African-American girl with long wavy black hair. She is an average sixth grader in her school subjects and her teachers like her because she is very compliant. Kendall's parents are very religious. In fact, her father is a pastor of the church he founded, and her mother is a missionary who takes trips at least once a year to Kenya, Africa. Both of her parents encourage her to sing in the church choir and usher on Sunday mornings. She reluctantly does these things as she knows that she will be under the watchful eyes of the congregation and be judged by everything she does or says.

Kendall is a little anxious about starting school at Rosebud Middle School. However, one small twinge of comfort is that she is coming up with most of her friends from Rosebud Elementary School. Kendall has one little brother named Cameron who is getting ready for kindergarten. She enjoys working with Cameron, and at times she babysits him while her parents take care of church business. She is currently teaching Cameron to read and write his name. He loves technology and already knows how to control an iPad and smart phone.

Kendall McSwain was anxious about the first day of school. She never had any problems making friends since she was so pretty and smart. However, she did battle with self-esteem issues due to her parents being pastors. She always had to watch what she did or said on most occasions and today was no different. Her mother and little brother Cameron said a prayer for her this morning as she left to board the bus. As Kendall searched for her class, a nice middle-aged Hispanic lady came to greet her. "Young lady, what class do you need to find?"

"I need to find mathematics with Mr. Ross." The nice lady pointed her to the west wing. "Thank you," Kendall replied.

As Kendall entered math class, she was surprised at the number of students she saw.

The class looked about thirty students deep, which was a change from Rosebud Elementary School's class sizes of no more than sixteen students per class. She perused the class for old faces. She did see Sophia Locklear, her American Indian friend who joined her parents' church over the summer, and Lyndsey Horne, her friend since kindergarten. They both attended Rosebud Elementary School with Kendall last year. Kendall felt a sense of relief when she could find a seat in between them both.

Sophia Locklear is an eleven-year old Native American girl who attended Rosebud Elementary School last year. She lived in the school district and knew most of the students who would attend Rosebud Middle School this year. She was not as nervous as some of her peers coming up to sixth grade.

Biologically, Sophia came from a strong family of farmers and business owners. Her grandfather owned the largest farmers' market in Bear Creek. All products were home-grown and organic. Both of her parents assisted with the family business. Her mother Shirley, did all the main duties and bookkeeping, while her father Phil, helped Sophia's grandfather with growing, caring for, and displaying and packaging the food for sale. On weekends, Sophia and her fifteen-year-old brother, Nathan, helped her parents by working the cash register or cleaning up the store to earn a little spending money.

At school, Sophia was considered average smarts, quiet, and a people-pleaser. She was always quick to give away her school supplies. She would often share her lunch money with other students. Her friends nicknamed her 'Sweet Sophia' because of her big heart. She was well-liked by her teachers and classmates.

Dolores Marrero is a Hispanic-American twelve-year old who came to the United States from Cuba when she was an infant. Her family is very closely knit, and this is how Dolores knows that she is loved unconditionally. She attended private school from kindergarten through sixth grade, but since her parents could no longer afford the payments due to their growing family, they enrolled Dolores in public school. While she is nervous about entering the seventh grade at Rosebud Middle School, she is also hopeful about the new friendships she will make.

Behind those wire-rimmed glasses is a bright and optimistic face of hope and an eagerness to learn. Dolores is very smart, being the proverbial "chopped from the same block" model of her mother. Like Dolores, Mrs. Marrero has a very high mental aptitude and used this talent to pull herself out of poverty in Cuba. She loved chemistry as a child and used her love of science and creating mixtures to forge a successful soap business when she was a young woman, which allowed her to raise enough money to move to the United States and earn her citizenship. Carlita Marrero is an inspiration to Dolores.

Dolores admires her father as well. Mr. Ruben Marrero is a car salesman who speaks so eloquently that he can convince a dog to jump off a meat truck. Mrs. Marrero sells her soap as a side hobby to assist her husband in making ends meet. Dolores loves her younger siblings; Maria who is entering second grade, and Tomas, who is entering fourth grade. During the school year, things could get a little chaotic in the Marrero household between homework, soccer practice, and preparing dinner, as all parties vie for the senior Marreros' attention. Dolores' family gives her a sense of pride.

Dolores' day started out very hectic as she was very particular about what to wear on the first day of school. At first, she chose a soft blue satin V-necked top with a pair of black skinny jeans. She thought that look was a little too hip for the first day of school, so she decided to wear a white and black polka dotted blouse with a pair of black slacks and black and tan wedge-heeled sandals. She left the house with confidence today.

"You look beautiful," her mother said as she was leaving.

"Great style, Sis," her siblings added. She loved her family. They gave her the assurance she needed to be herself and take pride in her Cuban heritage. Dolores was able to find her class, Computer Basics with Ms. Clark since the principal gave her family a tour of the school over the summer. Once she entered the classroom, she scanned the students through her wire-rimmed glasses for a friendly face. She decided to sit in the back of the class. "Hi, I'm Isabella," said the girl sitting next to her.

Isabella Newton is a very popular and sweet seventh grader at Rosebud Middle School. She is average in looks, height, and smarts. However, her bubbly personality put her in the top ranks in friendship. Isabella was a teachers' pet throughout elementary school and sixth grade. This is because she works very hard in school and stays out of trouble. Even though she is not the smartest student in the class, she always goes above and beyond what the teachers require of her. Isabella lives with her mom in the outskirts of Bear Creek. Since Isabella's mother applied for her to attend Rosebud Middle School, Isabella has to be driven to school every day.

Being an only child has its perks. Isabella has her own bedroom and doesn't have to share her bathroom with anyone. She can watch what she wants to on the television without any interruptions. She also can have as much as she wants to eat without any competition. Her mother, Angela, works very hard as a manager at Walmart. She loves her job and makes a reasonable income to provide for Isabella and herself.

Isabella decided to take Computer Basics to satisfy her love of technology. She took Basic Keyboarding last year in sixth grade but decided it might be a good idea to brush up on her computer skills. Isabella and Dolores liked each other right off the bat and knew they were meant to be fast friends.

Isabella and David had met each other at breakfast this morning. David was very enthusiastic about the first day of school because he would be in some of the same classes as Charlie Morrison, his best friend. David and Charlie attended Century Elementary together and when David moved away, he was disappointed about leaving his friends behind. To David's unexpected delight, he learned over the summer that Charlie and his family would be transferring to the Rosebud district. His father's business had relocated. Charlie would be attending Rosebud Middle School with him this year. Isabella and David learned that they both loved sports and would be trying out for softball and baseball, respectively, in the spring. David and Isabella also had math and Spanish classes together this year.

David Griffin is African-American and very smart. He is a twelve-year old seventh grader who transferred from Century Middle School to Rosebud Middle due to his mother getting a promotion on her job. They are able to move to the suburban neighborhood where Kai lives. David is quiet and a good listener. This nature was inherited from his mother who had to be a good listener because she was the oldest of seven children and didn't have a father figure in the home while growing up. David is a sounding board for his friends who felt like they couldn't talk to their parents. He never knew why he was trusted so much. He took it as a gift from God and treasured it greatly.

Despite insurmountable odds, David's mother went to technical school and earned a degree in banking and finance and went on to become a bank teller at Friends and Family Bank in Bear Creek. David has a younger sister named Angela who is in the fourth grade. David, who is more of a bookworm, is the opposite of Angela, who is an avid soccer player and loves the game of chess. She could beat just about anyone, young or old, at chess. Her dream is to one day become a world-famous chess player. David has dreams of success, too. However, he can't pinpoint exactly what he wants to do in life yet. This move to Rosebud was a little overwhelming for him. He wishes he could see his dad, who is away in Afghanistan for a one-year deployment.

The sixth graders had lunch first. They seemed so anxious about what to expect. There was a sense of relief for many of them since half of the day had already passed. Kendall showed no sign of anxiety since this morning. She acted as a leader helping several of the students with the process of getting their milk, lunch trays, utensils, and paying at the counter. She then sashayed over to sit with her friends Sophia and Lyndsey.

Kai and Jacob sat together at lunch since they had the same fourth period math class. Jacob was a ladies' man and many of the girls spotted him quickly. Kai felt important to be in the company of such a popular kid. Jacob embraced all this attention and added a little more swagger to his walk. Being an avid soccer player, Jacob had a very athletic build. Jacob had his eye on a cute brunette last year, but he did not want to make that common knowledge and lose the adoration of the many girls that had the hopes of him becoming their boyfriend one day.

As the first day of school ended, it was deemed a success. These students had high hopes for the start of this new school year. Teachers seemed to be nice and caring and their classmates, for the most part, were cool.

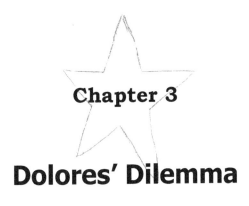

Chapter 3

Dolores' Dilemma

As the first weeks of school passed by, Dolores seemed to be faring very well with her teachers and classmates. She was very helpful with her siblings, Maria and Tomas, helping them with homework and assisting her parents with their household duties. Since Maria was in the second grade, she had little homework and it was usually completed within an hour. However, Tomas' homework was a little more challenging since he was in fourth grade and was learning how to do what they called the "new" math. Dolores did the best she could in helping both siblings as her mother prepared dinner.

While Dolores seemed to have it all together, she was hiding something from her family. Ms. Roy, her seventh period Math Function's teacher, was fairly new and shared with the class that she had only taught fifth grade for about two years in Canada before gaining her citizenship in the United States and being hired at Rosebud Middle School. Ms. Roy had long blonde hair, stood tall and slim, and looked to be in her mid-twenties. Dolores liked Ms. Roy but just could not understand Ms. Roy's accent or thought process.

One day, things began to spiral out of control. It was on the Friday before the first day of fall. Before class began, everyone was discussing what they would be wearing to the Bear Creek fall masquerade ball on Saturday night. The ball would be held to raise money for a larger football field. Isabella said, "I'm going to wear something unique, but you have to wait until the ball to see what."

Dolores said, "I will dress as a scientist because I love chemistry." Ms. Roy overheard Dolores speaking about her costume and said in a strong French accent, "Do you think a scientist is a good costume for the masquerade ball? What about something more appropriate, like a teacher or a waitress?" Dolores was shocked. Her mind raced with many thoughts. *Does she not think that I am smart enough to be a scientist? My mother has her own business, and may I add, a very successful soap business, and Ms. Roy probably uses some of the products. Why must I be a teacher or a waitress?*

Ms. Roy could tell by the look on Dolores' face that she had said something wrong. She apathetically said, "Oh, Dolores, don't take me seriously. I was just kidding around. You can be whatever you want."

Several of her classmates looked at how Dolores' face turned red and wondered what she would say next. Dolores only said, "Yes ma'am, okay."

Richard Brown whispered, "Dolores, don't be mad. Ms. Roy did not mean any harm."

Dolores conceded, but deep down inside she felt hurt and humiliated. She was a

Cuban American, and, at times, she thought that certain people felt as though she didn't stack up to the rest of her American peers. Ms. Roy was Canadian and had not been in the United States as long as Dolores had been. So how could she judge what was an appropriate costume for Dolores?

As the class came into session, Ms. Roy began explaining quadratic functions to the class. Ms. Roy wrote on the board, $f(x) = ax^2+bx+c,$ followed by several other equations. As the students began writing the formula and equations in their math notebooks, Dolores just could not let the comment from Ms. Roy go away. She could not concentrate on the math. Dolores raised her hand, "May I go to the restroom?"

Ms. Roy said, "Yes, you may."

When Dolores got to the restroom, her eyes began to water. She was so embarrassed about what Ms. Roy said, and most of all, that Richard Brown took Ms. Roy's side! She would be the laughing stock of the whole seventh grade. If they knew she cried, they would call her a baby. She just could not go back in the classroom right now. When about ten minutes passed, Isabella came to the restroom to check on Dolores. Dolores' face was red, and her glasses were completely blurred due to the tears that splotched upon the lens. Isabella tried to console Dolores, "Ms. Roy was not trying to be mean, she just probably never heard of someone dressing like a scientist at a masquerade ball."

Dolores said, "You're probably right. I guess I am just being a big baby." Dolores cleaned her glasses and dried her eyes and face. They both laughed and proceeded back to the classroom.

Dolores liked and respected Isabella very much. She was very pretty with long blonde hair and hazel eyes, and most of all, she was a very wise seventh grader. Dolores took pride in their friendship and looked forward to hanging out with Isabella this weekend at the masquerade ball. The best part was that Dolores' parents liked Isabella and Isabella's mother liked Dolores. That meant they could hang out without any major restrictions besides a 9:00 curfew. Dolores went back to the classroom and was able to finish the quadratic functions and get the homework for the weekend.

When class was over, Isabella and Dolores walked to their lockers together and parted their ways for eighth period. Isabella took Computer Basics and Dolores took chorus. Richard Brown, the handsome African-American guy from the math class, asked Dolores, "Are you feeling better?"

Dolores said, "Yes, thanks to Isabella."

"Good, because you are too beautiful to be mad." Dolores beamed with pride and began to get her confidence back, which was part of her family heritage.

At dinner that evening, Dolores shared with her parents what happened at school. Ms. Marrero was a great cook and knew how to season up their meals in that Cubano way that only she could. Dolores coyly looked up from her *arroz con polo* and fried plantains. Once she explained the situation concerning Ms. Roy and how Isabella made her feel better, her parents looked at one another. Mr. Marrero is a car salesman and had a way with words, knowing exactly what to say to make Dolores feel better. He said, "Never settle for less. If you want to portray a scientist at the masquerade ball, then do it. People will see what you are made of one day. Always be proud of who you are and never settle for less."

Tomas, Dolores' nine-year old brother, said, "Dolores, you need to be like me and make more friends. See, I have Chris, Larry, and Pedro as my friends. You only have Isabella. My teacher says that you should have more than one friend."

Ms. Marrero interrupted, "Tomas, be nice! Dolores has lots of friends. She is just quieter than others. Remember she is new to this school. She will make more friends in time."

Maria, Dolores' younger sister, chimed in, "Leave my sister alone, Tommy! She has lots of friends!" Dolores laughed inside at her little sister's defense.

Once dinner was finished and the kitchen cleaned up, Dolores felt better about the day. From Isabella's encouragement, Richard's compliment, her daddy's words to her sister's defense, she concluded that the day was not so bad. She was looking forward to the masquerade ball that she would be attending tomorrow night, and most of all, spending time with Isabella. She couldn't wait to see Isabella's costume. Once Dolores took her shower and began to wind down for bed, she pulled out one of her favorite childhood stories and read it until she fell fast asleep.

Chapter 4

The Masquerade Ball

Saturday had finally arrived. The kids were so excited about attending the masquerade ball which started at 6:00 sharp at the Bear Creek Country Club. They would get to show off their outfits and guess who everyone was. Pulling off the perfect look was of the upmost importance to the kids.

No one was more excited than Kendall. Kendall was so excited because she rarely got to do anything besides attend church events. She decided on dressing like a pop star because she loved to sing in combination with the glitz and glamour of stardom. She took extra time to make sure that her costume was not too flashy due to her parents being pastors. She truly had the good looks and stage presence to become a very successful superstar. Kendall glowed in her black leather outfit and high-heeled black boots. She let her long wavy braids sweep long behind her back. Wearing gold bracelets and earrings and just a touch of makeup, Kendall looked stunning.

Kai was excited about attending the ball because he was going as a ninja warrior. He was very interested in athletics and loved rock climbing and exercises that tested his endurance. He took karate classes and was eager to show off some of his new moves. His grandparents supported these efforts and took him to his weekly practice sessions. His sleek ninja costume fit him well.

Jacob loved sports which attributed to his fast connection with Kai. Jacob wanted to go to the ball as a soccer player, but he knew that his disguise would be blown, since practically the entire Rosebud Middle knew that he lived and breathed soccer. So, on a quick decision, Jacob decided that he would go as a baseball player. When Jacob was dressed, he had to admit that he truly looked the part.

David was another athletics buff. He loved track and field and, of course, baseball. However, he wanted to dress as a businessman because many of his friends would not believe that he knew how to dress so well. Since his dad was away for deployment in Afghanistan, David decided to borrow one of his dad's sleek business suits. He chose the charcoal gray double-breasted suit with a red and gray tie. He looked for his mother's briefcase, which would give David the look of a debonair entrepreneur. When he looked in the mirror, he smiled with pride.

Sophia chose a more traditional look and dressed as a teacher. She put on a white crisp-collared, button-up blouse and a navy blue mid-length skirt. Since she had a smartly-cut hair style, she only needed to add her mother's readers to complete the look. She carried a couple of notebooks and a pencil as props to accentuate her outfit.

Dolores dressed as a chemical scientist. Mrs. Marrero wore protective clothing when she created her soap mixtures, so it was easy for Dolores to find what she needed to create the perfect look. She wore a casual top with black slacks, a white coat, protective goggles, and rubber gloves. She carried a funnel and flask with colored water to simulate a chemical mixture.

Isabella was super excited about her costume! She decided at the last minute to dress as a princess. Determining which princess to dress like was a hard choice. Should she dress as a famous princess, like in the storybooks? Boy, did she love those graceful characters! In the end, she decided to dress as a random princess, so no one would recognize her. Preparing the princess look took some work. She decided to wear one of her mother's old pink bridesmaid dresses that needed some waist and length adjustments in which her mother helped her, a pair of summer white open-toed sandals, and a jeweled birthday tiara she received from her party last year that covered a chic updo hairstyle. Once Isabella was all dressed up and applied makeup, she felt extremely beautiful.

Shortly before 6:00, there was a hustle and bustle of students arriving at the Bear Creek Country Club. As parents dropped their children off, each student was greeted like a Hollywood superstar arriving at a movie opening to a crowd of admiring fans. Ballroom gowns, business suits, professional attire, sports gear, and chef jackets were some of the many different costumes available for all to see. There was an enormous amount of guessing on who wore these disguises. For the friends, they hardly had to guess about each other because most of them had shared what they would be wearing to the ball.

The setup of the country club was breathtaking. Glittering gold lights adorned the long rectangular tables covered with gold and silver table cloths. Spread from the center to the four corners of the ballroom were many round dinner tables covered alternately with gold and silver table cloths. The table centerpieces were long silver votives holding beautiful golden tea candles which floated on blue water. Each table held reserved seating for six students separated by sixth, seventh, and eighth graders who registered for the ball. On the right side of the ballroom was scrumptious food. The buffet tables consisted of salad, cheese pizza, chicken wings, macaroni and cheese, Salisbury steak, corn on the cob, and hot buttered rolls. The drinks available were sweet tea, fruit punch, coke, and water. For dessert, there was chocolate cake, apple pie, and banana pudding. The students were delighted about the delicious spread.

As the Rosebud Middle School students begin to fill up the ballroom, Principal Johnson and Mr. Rains entered the ballroom together. They were not dressed in costumes because they, along with the specials teachers, were serving as chaperones. Principal Johnson wore a black and white skirt and blouse set with black pumps. Mr.

Rains wore a navy-blue business suit. They kept a watchful eye on all the students as they mingled amongst one other.

Isabella and Dolores found their way to each other. Isabella knew right away who Dolores was because of her scientist disguise. Isabella complimented Dolores, "I love your outfit."

Dolores replied, "I love yours, too."

Isabella looked graceful and confident as she sashayed across the ballroom floor as a modern princess. She looked across the room for her friend David who shared her love of sports. She could not spot him just yet, even though she knew that he would be dressed as an entrepreneur. Isabella exclaimed, "I can't wait to see what everyone is wearing!" "Me either," Dolores agreed. They both giggled with excitement.

Sophia, Kendall, and their friend Lyndsey formed a huddle as they complimented each other on their costumes. Kendall looked amazing as a superstar, but she felt a little overdressed compared to Sophia who dressed as a teacher, and Lyndsey, who dressed as a politician. They all sat together at the reserved sixth grade table.

Kai and Jacob gravitated to one another. Kai felt special because Jacob was well-liked and attractive. Jacob liked Kai because he was athletic and fun, which reminded him a lot of himself. Them together in their baseball and ninja outfits made a super cool duo. Both boys walked to the tables to see who they would be sitting with. To their delight, they were sitting at the same table with David, Ronald, Isabella, and Dolores.

As the students approached their tables to sit, Principal Johnson welcomed everyone to the masquerade ball. "Welcome everyone. Have a good time and remember, the reason for this ball is to help raise money to build a new football field. I would like to thank all the teachers and students for coming. Please follow the same rules as you would at Rosebud, such as respect, responsibility, and personal space. You can begin making your way to the buffet tables in two serving lines." The teachers who taught specials served the students. The students chose their drinks as they came to the edge of the buffet table.

"Wow, everything tastes so delicious," stated Sophia.

"I know, right?" replied Lyndsey. "And I love the decorations. The principal really thought a lot about us to make everything so nice."

Isabella and Dolores overheard the girls talking, and Dolores said, "I am glad it turned out great. I was nervous when I first got here."

"Me too," agreed Isabella. "But when I got so many compliments on my costume, I knew the night would be prefect."

Kai and Jacob kept their heads down while they were eating, making no time for words. They were savoring every bit of the tasty morsels.

Once the students finished eating, it was time to enter the dance floor and guess who everyone was. Isabella finally found David and ran up to him and said, "David, I like your suit."

David responded, "Isabella, you look fantastic! Would you like to dance?"

"Sure," Isabella replied. As the two danced, they could see Jacob surrounded by a group of girl admirers, each competing for his attention. He had his choice of girls from sixth to eighth grade; however, he decided to dance with Charlene, a pretty seventh grade cheerleader.

Sophia, Kendall, and Lyndsey resumed their huddle by the wall while inspecting everyone on the floor, playing a guessing game of who each was dressed like. Kai danced with Naomi from his biology class. He looked sort of awkward in his ninja suit and Naomi in her doctor costume. Everyone seemed to be having so much fun as they danced late into the evening. The best part about the ball was seeing familiar faces, but not quite knowing them tonight.

As nightfall came, the parents began to arrive at the country club to pick up their children. Principal Johnson and Mr. Rains announced, "It is 9:30. The ball is ending. We hope you had a good time tonight."

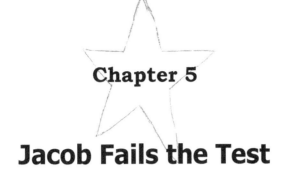

Chapter 5

Jacob Fails the Test

It was well-known around Rosebud Middle that Jacob Wentworth was handsome, smart, and athletic, and most of the boys and girls, popular or not, wanted to befriend him. Jacob portrayed himself as humble, caring, and willing to help someone in need. Although he was all of those at most times, he had one undesirable trait that brought some dismay to his teachers and parents. Jacob hated to study! He was very capable and even above average in intelligence, which allowed him to do well on most assignments even though he spent little to no time on studying or reviewing what his teachers taught him.

The end of the first semester was approaching and so was final exams. That meant Jacob would need to take exams for Biology 101, Algebra I, English/Language Arts, and Health & Physical Education. Jacob felt confident about his biology, algebra, and health classes, but English always gave him a run for his money. For reasons such as he didn't know when the assignment was due, or his little sister took his information, he could not get his research papers in on time, which resulted in him getting points deducted for being late.

Not only did he not turn in his research papers on time, he could not remember the difference between a run-on sentence and a dangling participle. He would say, "Why do you pronounce colonel the same way you pronounce a kernel of corn?" It just did not make sense to him sometimes!

Jacob's mother did all she could do to encourage him to study. She provided him with his own computer in his room and even checked out books from the library for him when she knew what his research topic was about. She knew that he was academically gifted but could not get him to take school seriously. After all, he was a ladies' man. His teachers adored him, including his English teacher, Mrs. Moss, who was willing to give him extra online assignments to help him better understand the more complex parts of speech. He *may* do them, he *may* not, depending on the type of mood he was in for the day.

Kai and Jacob would sometimes spend study hall together cramming notes and information before a weekly quiz or major test. Jacob admired Kai because he seemed to always have his nose in a book reading the latest Harry Potter novels. *If only I could be like Kai and study more, then I could make better grades in English*, he thought.

Thursday afternoon was a day of information overload as the teachers began with semester review. His biology teacher, Mr. Yen, gave the class a packet of key vocabulary words that the students needed to know by the final exam on Monday. Jacob was confident that he could learn all the scientific words with no problem. Kai and Jacob made plans to get together on the upcoming weekend to study the words together.

Algebra I was a breeze for Jacob. His algebra teacher warned the students that they needed to be able to solve equations using the distributive, communitive, and associative properties. "No sweat!" Jacob whispered to himself. He made all A's in the class this year and knew he would have no problems passing the final exam. Health and physical education class would not be a problem for Jacob because with him being an athlete, Jacob knew he could easily complete all the physical movements that Coach Lennox would dictate to the class.

English was a challenge for Jacob. He was barely passing, earning a C- on his most recent progress report. Mrs. Moss worked with Jacob by giving him extra assignments. However, since Jacob was so sporadic in completing the work, it barely improved his grades. Mrs. Wentworth met with Mrs. Moss on several occasions to see what was going on. Mrs. Moss informed Mrs. Wentworth, "Jacob is not completing his projects on time and does not put enough effort into his class assignments." Jacob knew it was important to keep his grades up because he wanted to remain the star player on the Rosebud Middle soccer team.

Mrs. Wentworth reminded Jacob to make sure he studied the final exam packet from Mrs. Moss over the weekend, which included parts of speech and a few reading passages from Shakespeare plays. Jacob had to explain how the characters felt in each scene. Jacob knew that he needed to pull up his grade or he would either lose his skateboarding privileges or be banned from attending the next football game with his friends. With the next football game being the last for the season, he knew he had to give it his best shot!

Jacob checked his locker to make sure all his study materials were in his bag and quickly made his way down the hall to speak to Charlene. Charlene was at her locker with a circle of friends surrounding her. Jacob was very interested in Charlene, and he made no secret of his affection towards her. Charlene obliged Jacob with her flirtatious brown eyes and the swing of her beautiful brown hair as she began to speak.

"Hey Jacob, I'm having a birthday party at the Burger Pit on Saturday at 12:00. Would you like to come as my date? I'm only inviting a handful of people, and I thought you might like to be one of the special few."

Jacob replied, "We have final exams next week, and I really need to pass to stay on the soccer team. So sorry, maybe next time."

Charlene looked somewhat disappointed, but she understood. She really liked Jacob and felt like a queen when he was around. "That's okay," Charlene said. "School comes first."

Jacob beamed with pride at Charlene's words. "By the way, happy birthday."

On Saturday morning, Jacob woke early and called Kai on his cell phone. Kai drowsily answered the phone. "Hey Jake," he mumbled.

"You up yet?" Jacob asked.

"Barely," Kai replied.

"Do you want to go to the library today to study in quiet away from our little brothers and sisters?" asked Jacob.

"I'll see if my mother can pick you up and take us both. Say around 12:00, will that work?" Kai asked.

"Ok, sounds good," Jacob assured Kai.

Jacob was determined that he was going to get that English grade he needed to stay on the soccer team. But he kept thinking about Charlene's birthday party and thought about how much fun it would be to spend some quality time with this kind and beautiful girl. His mind kept wandering back and forth about how much he wanted to pass English and how much he liked Charlene. He didn't want to let his mom down because she had fought so hard for him over the years to help him get through elementary school.

Jacob was very smart, but sometimes he had trouble staying motivated.

"Jake!" Mrs. Wentworth yelled. "Come finish breakfast with your sister. She has a soccer game this morning and we need to hurry. Kai's mother called and she is coming over in about an hour to pick you up so Kai and you can study. I like Kai, he is such a great influence on you."

"Okay, Mom!" Jacob rushed downstairs to a breakfast of pork sausage links, wheat toast and jelly, and orange juice. Kara was almost finished with her breakfast when Jacob came to the table.

"Jake, you are always late for breakfast," she chimed.

"Better late than never, little sis." Jacob loved his six-year old sister. She was so cute with her curly blonde hair and blue inquisitive eyes. Kara was an excellent soccer player, usually the one Coach Sanford called on when the team needed that last-minute goal.

Soon, Mrs. Wentworth and Kara were off to the soccer game. Mrs. Kem, with the twins in tow in the rear, was at Jacob's home to take both boys to the library. When she blew the horn, Jacob grabbed his books and jumped in the rear between the twin car seats. Kai was ready to jump right on into his notebooks and ace those finals. However, during breakfast, Jacob decided they would have other plans. "Goodbye, Mother," Kai beckoned.

"See you boys in about two hours," Mrs. Kem replied. Jacob and Kai jumped out of the car and headed inside the Bear Creek Main Library.

Once Kai and Jacob entered the library, Jacob shared his plan. "Charlene is having a cool birthday party at the Burger Pit right now. Since the place is around the corner, let's go for a little while and then come back to study."

Kai was reluctant about the whole thing. "What if our moms find out that we left the library and went to the party? Charlene's mom might tell on us."

"Aww, don't worry about that, I'll take care of our parents," Jacob reassured Kai.

"Well, *al-al-alright*, I guess," replied Kai. The boys arrived at the Burger Pit just as the party was underway.

Charlene spotted Jacob and beamed with joyful surprise. "Jacob! You made it! I am so happy! My party would not be the same without you!" Jacob gave Charlene an affectionate hug. Charlene took Jacob's hand and showed him off to her school friends. Kai stayed close behind the pair. Charlene was so excited as they played games and danced to the latest pop songs.

Charlene was showered with presents from her friends and family. Charlene's parents and little brother, Graham, made her feel so special today. The attendees had cheeseburgers, waffle fries, and soda pop. Jacob paid for Kai's meal since Kai was not part of the guest list. Charlene did not mind Kai coming because any friend of Jacob's was a friend of hers. The birthday cake was decorated with white icing and blue and pink flowers. It read *"Happy Birthday Charlene!"* in pink letters.

The time got away from Jacob, and they only had about five minutes remaining to get back to the library. As they were heading back, Kai's mother blew the horn at the boys near the crosswalk. "Hey boys, where are you two coming from? Get in the car. Kai has karate practice this afternoon."

"Just taking a little break from all this studying. We decided to take a stroll around the corner," Jacob lied. Kai was mum.

"Well, I hope you boys are ready for the finals on Monday," Mrs. Kem encouraged. She dropped Jacob off at home and she, the twins, and Kai rode off into the sunlight.

Jacob did not look at his English notes the entire weekend. Instead, he watched soccer videos on YouTube and played video games on his PlayStation, not giving his finals a second thought. The decisions that Jacob made cost him his English exam on Monday morning.

Exam time was here, and it was time for Jacob to prove to everyone, especially Mrs. Moss, that he could pass his final exams.

When Mrs. Moss gave him the packet, he could not remember half of the things that she went over about metaphors and similes during the semester, much less the vocabulary and questions from the passages he failed to read over the weekend. Jacob knew he blew the test and did not know how he would explain this catastrophe to his teacher, soccer coach, and, most of all, his mother.

Chapter 6

David Takes a Leap of Faith

D avid passed each of his exams with flying colors. He got his great attitude and intelligence from both of his parents, and his teachers liked him. He and his family were excited for the upcoming Thanksgiving and winter holidays. David and his fourth-grade sister, Angela, were grateful for a few days off from school. Their mother, Mrs. Griffin, who was a bank teller, was extremely busy as patrons were making a record number of deposits and withdrawals, preparing for holiday travels and gift-giving. She had to work longer hours throughout the week and even some half days on the weekends.

Lately, Mrs. Griffin did not pay too much attention to her children's moods because she was indulged in her recent workload. Amid the holiday busyness, David and Angela were missing their father. This would be the first Thanksgiving that Lieutenant Mark Griffin would not be with them to celebrate together as a family. Lieutenant Griffin had been stationed in Afghanistan for about eleven months and was due to come home before Christmas. However, David dreamed that his dad would be home for Thanksgiving.

One night, about a week before the holiday, Mrs. Griffin had a rare early night home and was preparing dinner for the family. David asked, "Mom, do you think Dad will be able to shorten his deployment so he can be home by Thanksgiving?"

Mrs. Griffin replied, "Well, it's hard to say. Usually soldiers can only come home early in cases of emergency."

"Wow," David replied. "I was hoping that he could be home with us to celebrate this year."

Angela, who was playing a single-player game of chess and mulling over her next move, quickly chimed in. "Yes, that would be great, but Daddy has to serve his time just like all the other soldiers. It would not be fair if Daddy said he would do it and then try to come home early."

Mrs. Griffin said, "Angie, your brother is not saying that Daddy shouldn't serve his time, he was just hoping that Daddy could come home early and spend time with us for the holidays."

"Sounds peachy, but it's nearly impossible," replied Angela.

Mrs. Griffin continued tossing the garden salad. She wistfully thought about her husband being home. It would be great to have Mark's help with the children, especially with David growing into a young man and Angela developing into a beautiful young lady. With Mark being deployed, she took on all the financial and emotional responsibilities of the home. Mrs. Griffin loved her children and wanted the best for them. Growing up, the former Lana *Brooks* (her maiden name) was the oldest of seven children. She remembered being the last one to get her plate at dinner time and usually the last one to be thought of when there were family functions.

Conversation during dinner was casual and light. When David had finished his dinner, he asked to be excused. Mrs. Griffin replied, "You may go upstairs while Angela and I tidy up the kitchen."

David wanted to spend some time alone and pray to God for his Daddy's shortened deployment. His parents taught him about prayer and often told stories of how their prayers helped them in many situations. At twelve, David did not really know how to pray because he did not do it often, but this was a time to pray the best way he could.

David kneeled by his bedside and uttered a small prayer that went like this, "Dear God, please make a way for my daddy to come home for Thanksgiving. I promise I will be good to my mom and sister while I wait for Daddy's arrival. Amen." That was all that David could think of at the time, and he hoped that it was good enough and God would answer his prayer. When he went to bed that night, he believed that some sort of miracle would take place and his dad would be home for Thanksgiving and stay for Christmas as well. He would keep the faith and hope for the best.

The next day, David wanted to hang out with his best friend Charlie Morrison. Getting used to a new school district has been somewhat easier due to Charlie's unexpected move to Rosebud Middle School. The boys made plans to catch the latest movie. David and Charlie's families had known one another since kindergarten and the parents trusted one another. Spending time with Charlie would ease David's mind a bit and take his mind off his dad's arrival time.

Charlie's mother picked the boys up and dropped them off for the four 'o clock matinee. The movie was an action-packed adventure of the evil villains versus the good guys. The proverbial ending was the good overcame the evil. For the most part, the movie was interesting and made a great addition to their huge bags of popcorn and oversized soft drinks. Mrs. Griffin picked the boys up from their outing. "Did you boys enjoy the movie?"

"It was amazing," answered Charlie.

"We thought it was great!" David agreed. Soon Charlie was home.

David noticed that his mother had a smirk on her face and asked, "What's up, Mom? What are you so happy about? I noticed that you have been smiling since you picked us up."

Mrs. Griffin replied, "Your father called today and guess what he told me?"

"WHAT?!" David was very hopeful that he was about to receive some good news.

"Well, it's possible that he may be able to come home early due to a ceasefire in Afghanistan where he is currently stationed. The general has made a request to the defense secretary for early dismissal of the troops."

David could hardly believe his ears! Could it possibly be true that his dad would be home for Thanksgiving after all? David remembered the prayer, and he tried hard to be good to his mom and his sister. Angela could be annoying at times, but he knew he had to keep his promise to God. David had faith that his prayer would come true. He began to think of all the things he and his dad would do together when he came home. As a young boy, before his sister Angela was born, David and his dad would go to the park and later go fishing. He recalled that one day he caught the biggest bass they had ever seen. It made a delicious dinner for them all that evening. He would love to go fishing with his dad again. David responded to his mother, "Daddy will be home for the holidays this year!"

Mrs. Griffin reluctantly replied, "We can hope for the best, but be ready for the worst, meaning, Daddy may not be home. The general is only making a request. That doesn't mean that they will be able to come home early."

"I know that, Mom, but I still believe that he will be able to be with us this Thanksgiving."

Thanksgiving Eve was here, and Mrs. Griffin was preparing all the fixings: turkey, ham, green bean casserole, rice and gravy, red beans, yams, and cornbread. Their home scented an herby aroma. David and Angela settled in the living room, entertaining themselves with a game of chess. They both could hardly wait to see their distant family members who came for the holidays. David's grandparents on his mother's side, Grandpa and Grandma Brooks, died in a fatal car accident when Angela was two years old, so the memories of them were fond but distant. Mrs. Griffin's siblings would bring the holiday desserts. Uncle Wayne would bring his famous peach cobbler, Aunts Vivian, Judy, and Connie would each bring a homemade cake, and Uncles John and Sam would bring pumpkin pies. It would be enough food to last for days.

Since Mr. Griffin was an only child, there was not usually much representation from his side of the family, except for the children's grandparents, Grandpa Griffin and

Grandma Griffin. They usually brought the ice cream and drinks. Thanksgiving was always a joyous day with family, and David longed for his dad to be with them like he always had been in years past.

As the evening began to wane, David knew that Thanksgiving Day was tomorrow, and there was no word on whether the general's request was approved or not. He did feel a little hopeless about the situation and decided to focus on the fun time of seeing his family and watching football with his uncles. *David knew he had prayed to God for his father's early arrival, and that's all he could do.* He went to bed and still faintly hoped that he would see his dad tomorrow.

It was Thanksgiving morning. David and Angela woke to the sound of their Uncle Wayne yelling to let everyone know that he was there and bellowed, "Now the party can begin!"

David's mother was already up and putting the finishing touches on the Thanksgiving meal. "Dave and Angie, come see your Uncle Wayne!" They both ran downstairs in their pajamas, still a little drowsy from their sleep. He gave them both a great big bear hug. Uncle Wayne looked great with his long, grey beard and grizzly mustache. He had a pot belly and strong arms, such a warm and caring man. He always spoiled them since Mrs. Griffin was his favorite sister. Uncle Wayne and Mrs. Griffin were the closest siblings since he was the second oldest Brooks child. They all loved Uncle Wayne very much! As usual, Uncle Wayne brought them gifts.

Mrs. Griffin opened a beautifully wrapped gift box. It was a glitzy gold-beaded bracelet. "Oh, thank you so much," she squealed with delight. "I love it! You've always had such good taste, Wayne!"

Angela opened a small gift box which contained a silver ring with her birthstone, an emerald. "Thank you, Uncle Wayne!" exclaimed Angela. "I can't wait to show it off to my friends at school!"

David received a gift bag containing a watch. It was a white gold watch with a brown leather band. David was ecstatic about the gift and gleefully said, "Thank you, Uncle Wayne. I love the watch and I love you."

One by one, all the family members began to arrive with their treats at the Griffin home. Mr. Griffin's parents came about an hour later with ice cream and soft drinks. They all complimented Mrs. Griffin on how beautiful the home was and how delicious the food looked. Her siblings looked up to her for guidance and support since she was now considered the family matriarch. Mrs. Griffin did a great job in keeping the family together after their parents' death by hosting family dinner parties and holiday gatherings. Her siblings relied on her approval before they made most decisions in life. They were a close-knit family unit who truly loved one another.

Soon it was time to set the table and place the turkey in the center for carving. Uncle Wayne was designated to carve the turkey this year since Mr. Griffin was deployed. Each family took their place at the table to prepare for the Thanksgiving prayer. David's mother asked David to say the prayer this year. David was a little reluctant about this because his dad usually conducted this prayer. Since David loved and respected his mom and did not want to disappoint his family, he proceeded to say a prayer.

When he was about to begin, a strange knock was heard at the door. All of the family members looked up in wonder. David silently hoped that it would be his dad. Mrs. Griffin went to open the door and a familiar voice said, "Lieutenant Griffin has been ordered to come home today."

Mrs. Griffin screamed with joy, "He's HOME!"

Everyone stood up, and they could not believe that Mr. Griffin was home from deployment early! Lieutenant Griffin looked tired and rugged, but still very handsome in his army uniform. His boots looked as though they had traveled a great distance.

Grandpa and Grandma Griffin began to cry with joy. "We would have picked you up if we had known."

"Don't worry. I was lucky that I was able to catch an Uber driver up to the corner and walk the rest of the way," exclaimed Mr. Griffin.

David was so overwhelmed! The prayer was put on hold, and everyone waited for Mr. Griffin to settle in and join them for Thanksgiving dinner. Even though Uncle Wayne was prepared to carve the turkey this year, he joyfully yielded the honor to Lieutenant Griffin. "You are the man of the house! Please carve the turkey."

David said, "This is the best Thanksgiving Day ever. God answered my prayer!"

Chapter 7

Sophia's Special Christmas Gift

As the winter holidays approached, there was a cheerful atmosphere at Rosebud Middle School. It was an exciting and festive time at school. A Christmas tree brought a festive mood to the front lobby near the office. Students and staff wore holiday attire that lightened the mood. The principals and teachers were looking forward to their two-week winter break, and the students were anxious about getting out of school and doing the things they liked without the thought of projects and homework. In two weeks, Rosebud Middle would be a ghost town.

Isabella was excited about her plans for Christmas this year and told her friend, "Dolores, I can't wait to visit the mountains this year. It will be cold but fun to hike in the snow."

Dolores replied, "Sounds like fun. We don't have any major plans, but I love the delicious Cuban dishes my mother makes during Christmas. She makes them only once a year, but I wish we could have them every day."

Kai asked Jacob, "Can we get together during the break?"

Jacob answered, "I dunno. My parents are thinking about taking a trip to Ohio so we can see our grandparents again. We haven't seen them in two years, and Kara has grown so much since then. Mom doesn't want them to miss too much time with the grandkids."

"I understand," Kai replied. "I'll find something to keep my little brothers occupied," he said with a sigh.

David was looking forward to spending time with his dad. "Charlie, have a great winter break. I'll be spending time with Pops at home. Maybe do some shopping and go to a few football games. I hope they don't call him back to deployment until after Christmas."

Charlie reassured David, "I'm sure God will allow you to spend more time with your dad before he has to leave. Just keep the faith. I think we're having a quiet vacation at home this year."

Kendall, Lyndsey, and Sophia were planning a girls' night during the break.

Kendall reminded her friends, "Don't forget to tell your parents that we are going to the movies this weekend." Sophia and Lyndsey agreed in unison.

By this point in the school year, Isabella and Dolores were the best of friends, as were Kai and Jacob. David and Charlie remained close throughout seventh grade. Kendall and Sophia had much in common since they attended the same church, and their friend, Lyndsey, completed the girls' circle of friends.

Mr. Ross gave the students a pop quiz in math class on fractions. After the quiz, the students could spend time using their inside voices talking with friends. Sophia finished her quiz and then waited patiently for her friends Kendall and Lyndsey to finish so they could talk. Their classmate, Marcella Rich, finished right after Sophia and looked around the room to see who she could talk to. Since Sophia sat so far away from Marcella, it was impossible. Both girls waited for the friends nearest them to finish before making conversation.

Soon Kendall was finished. After the girls turned in their papers, they began conversation. "So, Kendall, what are you doing during your winter break this year?" asked Sophia.

Kendall replied, "Oh, just directing the Christmas play at church and helping to feed the homeless with my mother's missionary group. Nothing fun, boring church stuff. And you?"

Sophia beamed with pride. "We plan to go to the reservation and attend a pow-wow with our extended family. Then we are having a special Christmas celebration at my house."

"Sounds like fun," Kendall said. "What about Nathan? Is he looking forward to winter break?"

Sophia replied, "All my brother cares about is girls right now. I never knew that tenth-graders could have such a one-track mind. Mama tells him to keep his eyes off the girls and in the books, ha, ha!" The girls shared laughter.

Once Lyndsey finished her quiz and turned in her paper, she joined the conversation. Lyndsey had a bubbly and positive attitude. She always added a spark of flair to the trio, from her small frame to her caramel skin and curly dirty-blonde mane. Lyndsey was mixed-race, having a Caucasian dad and an African-American mother, who just recently separated. Many could not figure out her race because she had blue eyes which she inherited from her dad and deep olive skin from her mother's side. Having a mixed heritage afforded Lyndsey the opportunity to relate to many people. That made her special. Lyndsey had a warm and caring demeanor that both Kendall and Sophia appreciated. Lyndsey was beautiful inside and outside, and Kendall and Sophia felt lucky to have her as their friend. She said, "Well, you both are welcome to come over my house for Christmas if you would like since my mother is all alone this year. You know, my parents are getting a divorce." Sophia and Kendall looked at each other in surprise.

Shortly after that, the class was over, and it was time for the sixth graders to go to lunch. As usual, the girls sat together. Sophia was still a little perplexed about what Lyndsey said about her parents. Sophia thought about how hard it would be if her mom and dad divorced. As she slowly wrapped her spaghetti around her fork, she hurt for her friend because she thought about Lyndsey being all alone and how she would not be able to see her dad as much as before. With Lyndsey being an only child, it had to be difficult not having your dad at home. Sophia couldn't fathom the idea of having only one parent live with her, especially during the holidays.

Lyndsey noticed Sophia's concern and reassured her. "Sophia, don't worry. My parents fight so much, it will be a relief to be with each parent separately on Christmas. I can choose which one I want to live with permanently when I turn sixteen in five years."

Kendall asked, "Who would you like to stay with if you had the choice?"

Lyndsey replied, "I really don't know. I love them both; I have five years to decide."

"Fair enough," said Kendall. "I'm so sorry for intruding."

Lyndsey comforted both girls. "Hey, you two, you are my friends. I don't mind it at all. The invite is open if you want to come over for Christmas. Just let me know and I will tell my mom." The girls finished their lunch with casual talk, and once the bell rang, they headed to their third period classes.

As Sophia continued down the hallway, she saw Principal Johnson redirecting some playful students back to class. Sophia thought, *Principal Johnson is very nice and cares for the students*. Principal Johnson tried to support the students and teachers however she could. She was well-liked by the parents throughout the community, and the super-intendent and other school principals often considered her one of the town's greatest leaders. Sophia knew she was blessed to have Principal Johnson and the assistant principal, Mr. Rains, as her administrators.

Sophia's mind began to wander back to the thought of Lyndsey's parents getting a divorce. It bothered Sophia because she really liked her friend's parents, and they seemed perfect for each other. Dr. Horne was a prominent pediatrician in Bear Creek. In fact, he was the family doctor for many of the students who attended Rosebud Middle. He was very tall and slim with dark hair. Mrs. Horne was a district attorney and well known throughout the community as well. She was of medium height and weight, and her hair was usually pulled back into a chic bun. With her gem-studded glasses and designer dress suits, she was the look of elegance and class.

In English class, Sophia could hardly concentrate on Mrs. Moss' review lesson. Her mind continued to go back to Lyndsey's parents. She recalled last summer when her and Lyndsey's families went to the Bear Creek Carnival. They had such a great time eating funnel cakes and pizza and getting on all the rides. She remembered how Dr. Horne convinced her to ride the monster roller coaster that even her brother Nathan was afraid of! She laughed inside when she thought about the shock on Nathan's face when she got off. She thought of the time she spent the night with Lyndsey, and the next morning, Mrs. Horne made them a yummy breakfast of French toast sticks, eggs, and waffles. It was one of the best breakfasts that Sophia ever had.

Then, Sophia had an idea. *Christmas is a couple of weeks away, and I have plenty of time to speak with my mother about doing this for Sophia. I will let Kendall know, but she will have to keep the secret to not blow the surprise. I will make Sophia a dream catcher. Why not?* Sophia thought. *If you dream about something you really want, the dream catcher will make it come true.* Sophia always used her dream catcher when she went to bed because she knew it would protect her from bad dreams and funnel in all the good dreams. "Lyndsey is probably having dreams of her mother and father getting back together." Sophia thought it was the perfect gift.

At the end of the day, as the girls loaded the school bus, Sophia sat with Kendall and said, "I'm getting Lyndsey a dream catcher for Christmas."

"Why?" Kendall asked.

"Because I think it will make her dreams about her parents getting back together come true. She loves and needs both parents," Sophia replied.

"Well, try it, you never know. I was looking at Lyndsey at Bible class last night, and she looked sad. Anything that can cheer her up will be great," Kendall agreed.

"Don't say anything about this to anyone," Sophia requested.

"Your secret is safe with me," Kendall replied.

Sophia's mother thought it was a great idea. As soon as Sophia and Nathan finished their homework and dinner chores, Mrs. Locklear took them out to their family store to grab wire, beads, yarn, ribbon, and feathers. Since Lyndsey's favorite colors were brown and blue, Sophia made sure she picked everything in different shades of blue and brown hues. Once she had all her materials together, she began working on the dream catcher until it was her bedtime. It took Sophia about a week to make the dream catcher, and when she finished it, it was a beautiful sight!

Soon, Christmas day had arrived. Sophia's family had plans to go to the reservation and participate in their annual holiday pow wow. This was a great time for Sophia to reconnect with her distant family members and meet new friends. She was looking forward to the singing, dancing, and eating of delicious foods. After getting dressed for breakfast, she and her family sat around the Christmas tree to open their presents. Sophia received a beautiful Native American necklace and earrings set from her mother. Her dad surprised her with a new bike. She loved the freedom she felt when she rode a bike. Her brother gave her a new pair of brown leather boots. They were nice! She loved all the gifts from her family.

Once the family had finished the gift exchanges, Sophia reminded them that they needed to stop by Lyndsey's house to drop off the special gift before heading to the pow wow. Nathan was a little slow this morning, but they were finally ready to go about an hour later. Sophia could hardly wait to present her gift to Lyndsey.

When they arrived at Lyndsey's beautifully holiday-decorated home, Sophia knocked at the door and Lyndsey answered. She looked pretty in her red and green dress; however, she seemed a little melancholy. Sophia chimed, "Merry Christmas!" and Mrs. Horne invited her in. "I have a special gift for you Lyndsey, but I can't stay because we are on our way to the reservation." Mrs. Horne and Lyndsey seemed very grateful for Sophia's thoughtfulness. She presented Lyndsey with the beautifully wrapped package.

When Lyndsey opened the box, she exclaimed, "It's beautiful! What is it?"

Sophia said, "It's a dream catcher. I made it myself, do you like it?"

Mrs. Horne replied, "It's the most beautiful piece that I have ever seen!" Sophia had to agree. The blue and brown beads and feathers gave the dream catcher an elegant look.

Sophia went on to explain the meaning of the dream catcher. "Lyndsey, the dream catcher will make your dreams come true. Sleep with it at night and the catcher will wash away the nightmares and fulfill your good dreams. I thought you and your mom may like it for Christmas."

Lyndsey was to the point of tears. She was so overwhelmed by the significance of the gift. "Sophia, thank you so much! I didn't get you a gift. I'm so sorry."

Sophia replied, "Your friendship means so much to me, and I want you to be happy, especially today. That's the best Christmas gift that you could ever give me!" Lyndsey beamed with happiness.

Sophia's family beeped the horn for her to come out so they would not be late for the pow wow. Sophia gave Lyndsey and her mother hugs and waved goodbye. "Merry Christmas!"

They both shouted, "Merry Christmas!" to Sophia as she left. Sophia was elated that she could bring some joy to the Horne's home. She jumped in the car and contently put on her headphones to enjoy her favorite tunes as they traveled to the reservation.

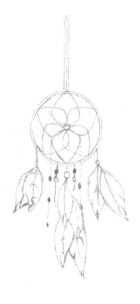

Chapter 8

Isabella, the Short Stop

If you had a conversation with Isabella Newton, she would tell you that her life was good. She had a wonderful mother, great friends, and teachers who really believed in her ability and tried very hard to push her to her greatest potential. Dolores was Isabella's best friend, and it was uncommon to see one without the other on any given day. Isabella was cute, well-liked, and smart. What more could she ask for?

The one thing Isabella dreamed of was making the girls' softball team this year. She loved watching baseball and softball in her spare time when her mother was working late hours at Walmart. She knew all the positions in softball and knew that this sport was the one for her. She talked it over with her friend David in computer class one day, and he encouraged her to try out for the spring season. "You should try out for the team," he said. "You will make a good short stop because you really know the game."

"I'll think about it. I need to talk with my mom first and see what she thinks."

Isabella was not worried that her mother wouldn't support her, since she always supported her in everything she did. Isabella remembered the time that she asked her mother for a puppy when she was in fourth grade. At first, Ms. Newton protested, but after much pleading, her mother gave in and surprised Isabella with a cuddly, little black Maltese. Ms. Newton trusted Isabella to care for the puppy properly and expected no less. Isabella did a great job with her puppy, whom she named Star, making sure she took her out for walks, fed her, home-trained her, and showed her love. Today, Star is a healthy young dog, and she and Isabella are the best of friends.

Softball is something different, however, thought Isabella. *It requires practicing after school, making the team, paying for a uniform and cleats, and some traveling for games.* As a Walmart manager, her mother worked long hours. During the past holiday season, Ms. Newton had to work double shifts because this Walmart was the only one in Bear Creek and people came from other small towns to shop there. Isabella did not want to add more stress to her mother's workload, but she really wanted to play softball this year and would ask her mother tonight during dinner.

At dinner that evening, which consisted of roast beef, potatoes, and green beans, Isabella had enough nerve to ask her mother about trying out for the softball team. Star rested in the kitchen on her little bed and looked on. Isabella explained, "They have try-outs next week, so I have to get my sports physical done before then."

Ms. Newton replied, "I will try to arrange the appointment with the clinic and see if Dolores' mother wouldn't mind taking you since I must work. Other than that, it is fine with me."

"Thank you, Mom!" Isabella squealed. She was so happy she could barely finish her dinner. Once Isabella finally finished her last bit of beans, she offered to wash and dry the dishes without her mother's help to show appreciation of her mother's support. Isabella loved her mother very dearly and was glad that she could always count on her mother to be in her corner.

The rest of the week passed by quickly. Isabella could not wait to try out for the team. She told her friends Dolores and David about the good news in computer class. "I get to try out for the softball team." David encouraged her, "Well you should make the team since you know all about softball and you played in Bear Creek Little League when you were younger."

"I know," Isabella exclaimed, "but that was so long ago, and I don't know if I can still hit a ball, much less catch one."

David replied, "You won't know until you try."

Dolores agreed, "Just like Mom said on the way to the clinic, you have to believe in yourself before others will believe in you."

"Thanks, guys," Isabella said.

Rosebud Middle School was the center of much buzz about who was trying out for spring sports such as track and field, tennis, golf, volleyball, baseball, and of course, softball. Coach Lennox had the list of the dates and times of where the softball practices would be held. Isabella saw that Jacob and David were both trying out for the baseball team this year. The first softball practice was scheduled for today at 4:00 on the baseball field. Isabella was excited but a little nervous at the same time. However, she loved softball and could not wait to practice.

After the last bell rang for dismissal, Isabella rushed to the gym to change into her softball gear. Since the school colors were blue and red, she wore red and blue cleats to match her shirt, shorts, and knee pads. She grabbed her helmet and glove from her gym locker. Isabella looked the part as Coach Lennox took roll to make sure all the prospective players were present and accounted for.

He began to call the roll, "Watts!"

"Present!" Mary Watts answered.

"Jones!"

"Present!" Cindy Jones replied.

"Brighton!"

"Present!" Valerie Brighton answered.

"Parker!"

"Present!" Angela Parker answered. Cherie Alexander, Lisa Smith, Jennifer Williams, Sarah Lloyd, Terrie White, Wendy Zaldana, and Soo Mae Lee were all present and ready for practice.

Finally, he called, "Newton!"

"Present!" Isabella replied with relief.

After calling the roll, Coach Lennox explained, "Since there are only twelve trying out this year, you can all make the team if you show good effort. The battle will be over who gets the starting spots. This depends on each player's skills." Isabella hoped that her skills were good enough to get her a starting position. Any starting spot would be good enough for her.

The first day of practice went smooth. Isabella hit a long ball out and made a couple of catches. She had to slide one time to third base which caused her to get a little dirty. Wendy served as the umpire and was able to tag a couple of the girls out. Isabella was surprised at how fast Terrie and Sarah could run! They were able to avoid getting tagged at third base and each scored a homerun.

Coach Lennox watched carefully during the practice innings and took notes on each girl's actions. He looked pleased with what he saw. He looked to be in his mid-thirties and very athletic. He sported a bald head which intensified his green eyes. Coach Lennox was the head coach at Rosebud Middle School where he had been a staple for fifteen years now. He coached football, track and field, and the girls' softball team. Soon practice was over, and he told them that they would meet tomorrow after school at the same time and place. "Great job today, girls!" he assured them as they headed out to the front of the building to meet their parents.

Isabella felt great about today's practice, and she talked about it all the way home, at dinner, and while doing her homework. "I can hardly wait for practice tomorrow." She watched contently as her mother patiently listened and washed Isabella's practice uniform. "You just might be a starter, Izzy, especially if practice went as well as you said it did," Ms. Newton encouraged.

"I will keep my hopes up," replied Isabella. "Coach Lennox is posting the kids who made the positions at the end of the week."

The practices continued on throughout the rest of the week. Each of the girls who practiced wanted to be a starter on the Rosebud Middle softball team. Isabella knew it was tough competition because Jennifer Williams could throw a fast ball like nobody's business and most knew that she was a sure pick for pitcher. Terrie, Sarah, and Angela were vying for the three base positions. Wendy did a great job as umpire and word was already out that she would get that position. Isabella wanted to be shortstop but would have to beat out Valerie Brighton in the running. Finally, the outfielder and catcher positions were up for grabs. Isabella did not feel as comfortable catching balls, so she really did not want those positions unless she had to take them.

Monday was finally here! The spring sports list of finalists was posted in the front lobby. While Isabella was in her first period class, she asked Dolores to come with her after the bell rang to see if she made the list. Isabella told Dolores, "I am very nervous. I wonder what position I qualified for and if I'll be a starter." She had Dolores look first. Dolores looked at the many lists.

Dolores placed her hand on each list looking for the right one: *Tennis, Track &*

Field, Golf, Baseball, finally *Softball!* "I found it!" shouted Dolores.

"And?" asked Isabella.

"Wendy Z.- Umpire, Jennifer W.- Pitcher, Terri W. – First Base, Sarah L.- Second Base, Angela P.-Third Base, Mary W.- Catcher, Isabella N.-Short Stop."

"Are you serious? I made short stop!!!!" shouted Isabella. She could hardly believe it.

"Don't you want to hear the other positions?" Dolores asked. *"Lisa A.- Outfield 1, Cherie A.- Outfield 2, Valerie B.-Outfield 3. Soo Mae L.- Rotating Pitcher."*

Isabella tuned out the other names even though she was happy for them, too. Many other students surrounded the lists in the lobby, and she could hear the sounds of excitement and disappointment of some. She saw Valerie and congratulated her on making the team. "Way to go, Valerie!"

"Let's get to class, Dolores. We are already running late. Thanks for checking for me." Isabella walked to class, still in disbelief that she made the softball team and would be the short stop! She couldn't wait to get home to tell her mother the great news!

Chapter 9

Kendall Makes a New Friend

Kendall was a popular sixth grader at Rosebud Middle School. She was beautiful and very chic, usually wearing the latest fashion trends and styles. With her flawless, dark skin and long wavy braids, she was an attractive sight to behold. Kendall had several male admirers, whom she did not afford the satisfaction of a second look. Her closest friends, Sophia Locklear and Lyndsey Horne, looked up to her and felt honored to be in her presence. They imitated her and tried to dress like her.

Kendall was an average student, but her teachers liked her because she always did her classwork and homework and turned in her assigned projects on time. She was very respectful to her teachers, which they attributed to her religious upbringing. Most knew that Kendall's parents were very active in their church; her father was a pastor and her mother was a traveling missionary. She was an active member in her church and the epitome of a well-rounded child.

It was very common to see Kendall surrounded by a flock of people. Even though she had two best friends, she had several other girls who wanted to be a part of Kendall's circle. Marcella Rich was one of them. She was nice enough and liked by Kendall's friends. However, it was clear to the trio that Kendall was Marcella's favorite. Like Kendall, Marcella was African-American. She was brown-skinned with a short afro. She dressed casually every day, usually wearing faded jeans and white sneakers. Most would say that she was far from attractive. Marcella had difficulty making friends; however, she did manage to forge a friendship with Rhonda

Russell, another African-American girl, who was in most of her classes.

One spring day, as the students were leaving second period and heading to the cafeteria for lunch, Marcella saw Kendall at her locker and thought, *Now's my chance to talk to Kendall without the others around.* "Hi Kendall," Marcella said.

"Hi Marcie. *Wuzzup?*" Kendall replied.

Marcella asked, "Just wanted to see if you would like to hang out with me at the movies this weekend? There's a great Disney movie playing right now that I think you might like. My treat." Kendall was a little surprised by the invitation because she did not really know Marcella any more than just seeing her around elementary school and now just in her math class with Mr. Ross.

"Well, I don't know. I have to help my parents with church stuff on Saturday, and then I sing in the choir on Sunday. I'll have to let you know tomorrow," Kendall chimed.

"No problem," stated Marcella. "Just let me know."

Soon Sophia and Lyndsey caught up with Kendall, and they walked to the cafeteria together. "Hey girl, I saw Marcella speaking with you. What did *she* want?" asked Sophia. Lyndsey was all ears, too.

"She asked me if I wanted to hang out with her at the movies this weekend," Kendall responded.

"I thought you were helping your mom with the women's group this weekend with my mom," Sophia said.

Kendall replied, "I told her that. I'm not sure if I want to hang out with her though. She seems a little weird."

Lyndsey agreed, "I know. She doesn't seem very friendly, either."

Kendall chimed in, "I just don't know if I want any more friends. I already have you two. My mother always told me a person with too many friends will quickly come to ruins."

Sophia replied, "I don't think one more friend will bring you to ruins. You should give her a chance."

Lyndsey jeered, "That's why we call you 'Sweet Sophia,' because you always look at the bright side of everything."

Kendall defended Sophia. "And we love you that much more for it!"

When Kendall got home after school, her little brother Cameron greeted her at the door. "Kendall!!" Cameron jumped up and down and grabbed his sister's legs. Kendall gave her little brother a kiss on the forehead. Cameron was so bright-eyed and enthusiastic about school. He was in kindergarten and he loved his teacher, Miss Gardner. He always talked about some fun thing they were doing, whether it was studying apple seeds or building a gingerbread house. Kendall missed those days when life was such a breeze. Middle school required so much work, and she barely got a chance to breathe. Cameron went back to working on his spelling homework which was due tomorrow.

Kendall's mom was in the dining room working on some pamphlets to prepare for the women's group activity on Saturday. She looked up excitedly when she heard Kendall enter. "Hi, dear daughter, how are you today?"

"Fine, Mom. How was your day?" Kendall responded.

Her mom said, "Oh, you know, just a little of this and a little of that. Went to the market to buy a few groceries, then went to the craft store to buy some items for Cameron's insect diorama. Just an ordinary day. Enough about my day. How was school today?"

Kendall replied, "I had a great day. Passed my math test and I think I passed my science quiz. Mr. Yen can be tough sometimes in biology, but I think I did alright. By the way, Marcie asked if I could hang out with her at the movies this weekend. I told her I would have to see before I gave her an answer. We have the women's group on Saturday and church on Sunday."

Her mom said, "I don't know Marcie or her family, so maybe if your father and I went with you two, it may be alright on Friday. Only if you want to."

Kendall responded, "I don't know if I want any more friends since I already have two besties."

Her mom replied, "Always accept friendship when it comes. You don't want too many friends, but making new friends is a great experience. In order to have friends, you must show yourself friendly, according to the Bible." That made sense to Kendall. She was glad that her mother cleared up things for her. Mrs. McSwain headed to the kitchen to prepare tonight's dinner.

Sylvia Wright McSwain was such a blessing to all who knew her. The third child of seven, Sylvia was raised in a staunch Christian home. Her parents were both very religious, and they ensured that all of their children followed the Bible's laws to the tee. The family was not allowed to watch television or participate in many extracurricular activities. However, when Sylvia and her siblings grew older and had families of their own, they maintained their religious values, but were a little more lenient with their children.

Kendall looked up to her mother and wanted to be just like her when she grew up. She admired the way her mother helped people in need with her missions group and traveled overseas to minister and provide supplies to people in Africa.

Her dad, Pastor Tony McSwain, had arrived home from a group meeting with his deacon board by the time the table was set. He was a very hardworking and supportive father. She thought how handsome he was with his clean-cut face and tall, muscular build. Kendall admired how her dad kept his ever-growing ministry in tact while skillfully balancing his household duties. He looked dapper in his business suit as he checked over Cameron's homework.

As the family sat down to dinner which consisted of fried chicken, mashed potatoes and gravy, green beans, and cornbread, Kendall had another question for her mother. "Mom, what if your friends don't approve of the person you want to be friends with?"

Her mom answered, "Sometimes people have to grow on you. If they see how you interact with Marcie and know that you have accepted her, they will have to get on board with it or they will be the ones sitting on the outside looking in."

Her dad added, "Kendall, you have to use your own mind, make your own decisions. In the end, only you can decide who you want to be your friends." That helped Kendall make up her mind. She knew exactly what she would tell Marcie tomorrow.

The next morning, Kendall met Sophia in the library. They were catching up on some assignments for English class. On the way out, Kendall told Sophia, "I'm going to get Marcella's phone number and get to know her some first before hanging out with her just yet."

Sophia replied, "That's good. You don't really know her too well and your parents need to know her some first, too."

Kendall agreed, "That makes sense. My parents really helped me make up my mind.

It's good to make new friends, but in the end, it's all up to me."

Right after English class and on the way to their lockers, Kendall approached Marcella. "Hi Marcie. Let's exchange phone numbers. I won't be able to go to the movies this weekend, but maybe some other time."

Marcella said, "No problem, I understand. Do you have your phone ready?" Kendall pulled out her cell phone, and she and Marcella exchanged phone numbers. "Can I call you this evening?" Marcella asked.

"Sure, after seven. I have to do home-work and eat dinner and then we should be able to talk a little afterwards." Both girls were pleased as they headed to the cafeteria for lunch.

Chapter 10

Kai and the Karate Match

Kai was a very athletic and charismatic young man. His seventh-grade year was going well. He was making good grades and keeping them up during his busy sports-filled life. This past winter, he was very active in wrestling. As the spring arrived, Kai began participating in his all-time favorite sport—karate. The best thing about Kai's life was that his family was very supportive of him in middle school. With his mother being a full-time parent and his dad being an aeronautics engineer, they did their best to attend all his wrestling matches as well as any other activities he chose to participate in.

Kai had the luxury of both grandparents living with the family. They moved in with the Kems when Kai was six years old, mostly to help with the twin boys. This meant that Kai's three-year old twin brothers had plenty of attention when they were home and Kai could get a decent proportion of his parents' time and support when he needed it. Kai was a good brother, always willing to spend time with his brothers, feed them, and give them baths. Kai had great affection for the twins, and they loved their big brother very much.

It was a busy time at Rosebud Middle School with many of the students getting ready for the second half of the school year, hoping to fill it with interesting activities to get them through. Kai had been taking karate lessons since he was in second grade, so he was looking forward to getting back into the swing of things. He enjoyed the thrill of the karate competitions and earning new belts. Right now, Kai was at a purple belt. The purple belt stood for changing the sky of dawn. This time around, he was hoping to move up another level to a brown belt.

Kai's karate instructor, Michael Crenshaw, owns the main karate center in Bear Creek. He is a seventh-degree black belt who has been training students for over twenty years. He had earned several awards for his karate skills and for his dedication and support in the community. Mr. Crenshaw was also known for his strict and no-nonsense teaching tactics and high expectations for his students. Because of this, Kai was very disciplined and controlled in his craft.

Today at school, Kai met up with his best friend Jacob in between classes. The boys had formed a tight bond over the past few months. With Kai being new to Rosebud Middle School, it was great to meet someone as popular and charismatic as Jacob. Jacob was a positive person and always encouraged Kai in all his endeavors. Jacob was grounded from playing spring sports because he failed his first-semester exams. The Wentworths were sticklers for their children making good grades and cared a great deal about their education. Since Jacob couldn't participate in sports right now, his closest proximity to any athletics was Kai's karate matches.

"Jacob, did you know that Isabella made the softball team this year?" Kai asked.

"Wow, that's great! I know she really wanted to be on the team. What position did she get?" Jacob asked.

"I think she made short stop. Dolores was talking about it in computer class yesterday. We need to go check her game schedule so we can support her next time."

"That sounds like a plan."

Kai continued, "You know, I have my karate match tonight. Think you can come watch?"

Jacob replied, "Let me check my schedule. I know I have some English work to do. Mrs. Moss won't let up. I'm so over that class! Can't wait till it's over."

"I know what you mean. She is so particular about everything. But if you can make it, my match is at eight o' clock."

"Ok, buddy, see you next period," Jacob assured. The boys exchanged handshakes and went to their respective classes.

When Mrs. Kem picked up Kai from school, she reminded him that he had karate practice, so he needed to hurry and get his homework done. "I need to pick the boys up from daycare after I drop you off. How was your day at school?"

"It was great, Mom. Mrs. Roy gave us some polygon equations to work with tonight. I have to go back and look over the notes to get it right," Kai responded. "Oh, by the way, Isabella Newton made the softball team."

Mrs. Kem beamed. "That's great! I know she's excited." When they arrived at the house, Kai ran in quickly, grabbed a cinnamon roll and some apple juice, and worked diligently to complete his homework.

About an hour later, Kai was all ready to go, dressed in his karate attire, including his purple belt. Mrs. Kem dropped Kai off to the karate center and reminded him that she would be back right after she picked the boys up from the day care. "Your dad should be here as soon as he gets off work," she assured Kai. "I'm proud of you, son." Kai beamed proudly at his mother and walked into the center full of confidence. He always enjoyed his karate sessions.

When Kai entered the large room, he saw some of his sparring buddies already warming up in the ring for today's practice session. One boy, Steven Krowosky, was of great interest to Kai. Steven was a tall blonde fast hitter and leg mover who earned a brown belt. He seemed a little cocky and always bragged about how much better he was than the other contenders. He was the only one with a brown belt, and he was quick to let the others know it.

"Hey dudes, y'all know that I'm the biggest and the baddest karate student out here," Steven boasted. "Just try to challenge me and see if you don't be picking up your teeth from the floor. I'm the only one with a brown belt now, and I will be moving up before all you losers!"

Kai thought, *If someone could beat him one day, he will shut up.* The other boys let Steven run on and on with his mouth until Mr. Crenshaw told him to be quiet and remember the code of conduct for all karate experts. Be brave, be bold, be respectful. Kai held these tenets close to his heart.

Mr. Crenshaw called the sixteen students to attention. He was a middle-aged, lean but muscular African-American man with a boxed haircut. He was very pleasant but required his students to practice hard and push themselves to be the greatest karate experts that they could be. He taught his students all the karate they knew, since he was the most sought-after instructor in all towns south of Bear Creek. "As you all know, we have our trial karate competitions tonight. I need each one of you to be prepared to contend against whom I assign you," Mr. Crenshaw chimed. "The best fighters tonight will move on to the final round on Saturday." His students were at mixed ability levels: three students with green belts, seven students with blue belts, five students with purple belts, and one student with a brown belt (Steven, of course).

Mr. Crenshaw pushed his students hard because he knew that most of them had the desire to become karate masters. He was strategic in assigning student pairs who had similar skill and ability to keep the practice rounds fair. Kai was one of the strongest purple belts, and only one of the five at this level would be able to pair with Steven. As Mr. Crenshaw began calling off names, Kai was a little nervous that he might be chosen to challenge Steven. "Miguel Ferrara and Kim Yong, Jared Jones and Wesley Poole, Sam Parker and Ty Nyuen..."

After Mr. Crenshaw had finished matching up the green and blue belts, he came to the last six students: five purple belts and one brown belt. The boys wondered who had to match up with Steven. Kai had mixed feelings about the situation. Kai thought, *I could defeat Steven if I had to fight him, but if I don't have to, it will be okay.* The instructor went on, "Roland Scott and Robert Gonzalez,

Mark Cole and Steven Krowosky, Kai Kem and Ashton Perkins." *Whew! Kai* thought. He wanted to move up to a brown belt, but he didn't want to challenge Steven to do it.

The practice session continued as each pair challenged. It was interesting to see how some of the boys were more flexible and disciplined than the others. For example, Jared and Wesley (both purple belts) seemed to be an odd matchup. Jared displayed his foot sweep with such ease and grace, while Wesley had poor timing with his knee strike. Roland could do the front roundhouse kick with more grace than anyone in the group, while his challenger Robert showed a choppy knee strike. As Kai looked on, his parents entered with the twins. They arrived just in time as it was Kai's turn to enter the ring.

Ashton was a very disciplined purple belt, but Kai knew his own moves and skill could overcome Ashton. Kai looked over at his parents with the boys in the stands, and they were waving at him and giving him thumbs ups. This encouraged Kai to put his best foot forward. Kai used forearm blocks, round-house kicks, and knee strikes to oppress his opponent. Ashton pressed Kai with stomp kicks, front kicks, and roundhouse kicks. The match went on for about fifteen minutes, and there was still no clear winner. Mr. Crenshaw stopped the match and told both boys he would have to analyze their moves on the video before he could decide a winner of the match. Since it was getting late, he decided to dismiss all the other contenders.

Kai was sweating profusely after the match and was hoping that he would come out as the clear winner. He noticed how much Ashton had improved over the course of practice sessions. Ashton was a stocky redhead with a very pleasant attitude. However, when it came to karate, he had a practical demeanor. His motto was "fight hard and win the game." Kai appreciated the resilience in Ashton.

When most of the students had left for the evening, Kai's dad met with Mr. Crenshaw. Mr. Kem asked, "So what do you think, Mr. Crenshaw?"

Mr. Crenshaw responded, "I will need to let you all know in the morning once I get a chance to review the video."

Mr. Kem replied, "Kai really wants to move to the next level and earn his brown belt."

"Kai is doing a great job, and I have no doubt that he will earn the belt. He just has to be able to compete in this round, and he will be fine," Mr. Crenshaw replied. Mr. Kem seemed satisfied, and both men went their separate ways.

On the way home, Kai seemed a little disappointed. Mrs. Kem tried her best to cheer him up. "Don't feel so bad, Kai. You may get chosen for the match. It will be okay. Either way it goes, you did your best. Don't you agree, honey?"

Mr. Kem bellowed, "Kai will get his brown belt. He was definitely the best fighter in that ring tonight!" The twins were very playful in the back seat. Kai wanted to put the whole thing out of his mind. *If he was chosen, fine, if not, fine, too.* He decided to think about his computer class project that was due on Monday.

As the family entered the home, the phone was ringing. Kai ran to answer it as his parents struggled to bring in the active twins and the Chinese takeout they would have for dinner. It was Mr. Crenshaw. "Hi, Mr. Crenshaw," Kai said.

Mr. Crenshaw excitedly responded, "Kai, get ready for the match on Saturday! You are the clear winner. Once I saw the video, I could not deny the fact that you were the most disciplined and skilled purple belt that I have. That also means that you will have to challenge Steven on Saturday. Can you handle it?"

"I sure can!" Kai beamed. "Looking forward to it!"

Kai hung up the phone and shared the good news with his parents. They were so amazed that they found out before the evening was over. Mr. Kem reminded him, "Keep the faith, and you never know what might happen." Kai thought about what his parents said and knew that he needed to be more patient and optimistic even in the most challenging situations. *Now, to only beat Steven...*

About the Author

D r. Sharonne Simmons is an up and coming author who has been a professional educator for over fifteen years. Her love for children has inspired her to write a series of books geared toward middle school students. The characters in *Kid Stars*

Rising remind her of the people whom she has encountered throughout her years of teaching school.

Dr. Simmons earned a Bachelor of Science in Education and a Master of School Administration at Fayetteville State University in Fayetteville, North Carolina, and a Doctorate in Education from Gardner-Webb University in Boiling Springs, North Carolina. In addition to teaching, she has served as an elementary school administrator. She resides in Fayetteville, North Carolina with her husband, son, and Milo, their orange tabby cat.

Kid Stars Rising

Kid Stars Rising showcases the adventures of seven students who attend Rosebud Middle School in Bear Creek. From Dolores' dilemma with her math teacher to Kai depending on his faith to face a strong challenger in karate, this reading experience is filled with ups and downs in the lives of these middle school students. During the topsy-turvy events they encounter, it brings the seven stars closer together and forms an unshakeable bond between them. Friendships are tested and proven, and the power of prayer, faith, and resilience will see them through in the end.